FIRST GRAPHICS

MANNERS MATTER ON A FIELD TRIP

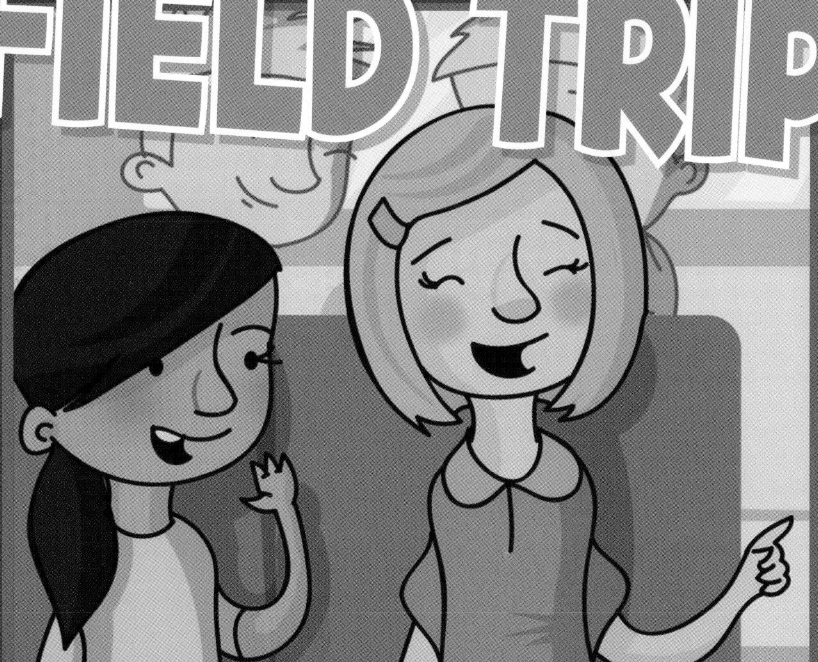

BY LORI MORTENSEN

ILLUSTRATED BY LISA HUNT

CAPSTONE PRESS
a capstone imprint

First Graphics are published by Capstone Press,
1710 Roe Crest Drive, North Mankato, Minnesota 56003.
www.capstonepub.com

Books published by Capstone Press are manufactured with paper
containing at least 10 percent post-consumer waste.

Library of Congress Cataloging-in-Publication Data
Mortensen, Lori, 1955–
  Manners matter on a field trip / by Lori Mortensen ; illustrated by Lisa Hunt.
    p. cm.— (First graphics manners matter)
  Includes bibliographical references and index.
  ISBN 978-1-4296-5331-2 (library binding)
  ISBN 978-1-4296-6225-3 (paperback)
  1. Student etiquette—Comic books, strips, etc. 2. School field trips—Comic books,
strips, etc. I. Hunt, Lisa (Lisa Jane), 1973– II. Title. III. Series.

BJ1857.S75M36 2011
395.5—dc22

                              2010028912

Editor: **Shelly Lyons**
Designer: **Juliette Peters**
Art Director: **Nathan Gassman**
Production Specialist: **Eric Manske**

Printed in the United States of America in North Mankato, Minnesota.
012012   006552R

TABLE OF CONTENTS

LET'S GO!

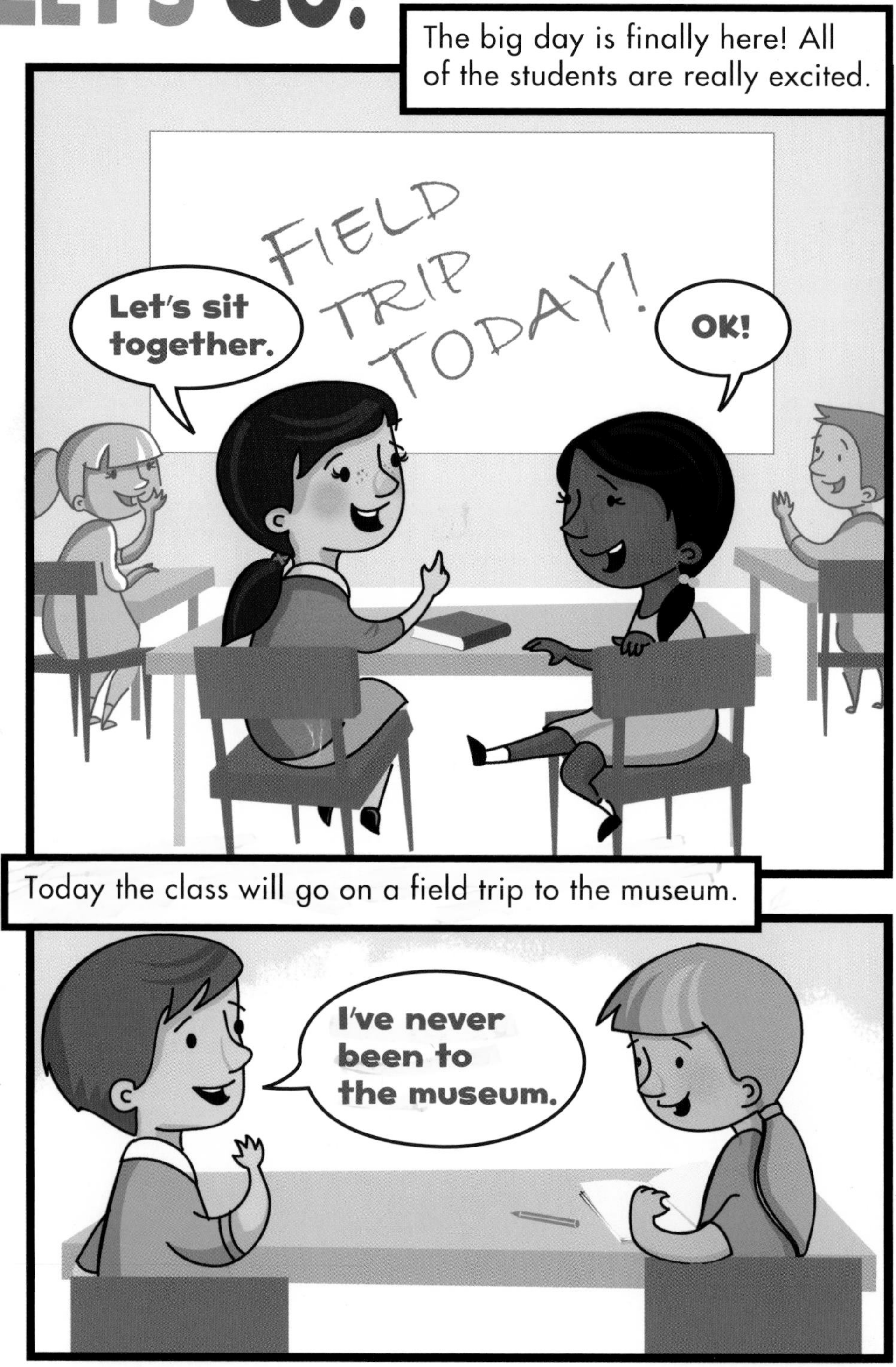

The big day is finally here! All of the students are really excited.
FIELD TRIP TODAY!
Let's sit together.
OK!
Today the class will go on a field trip to the museum.
I've never been to the museum.

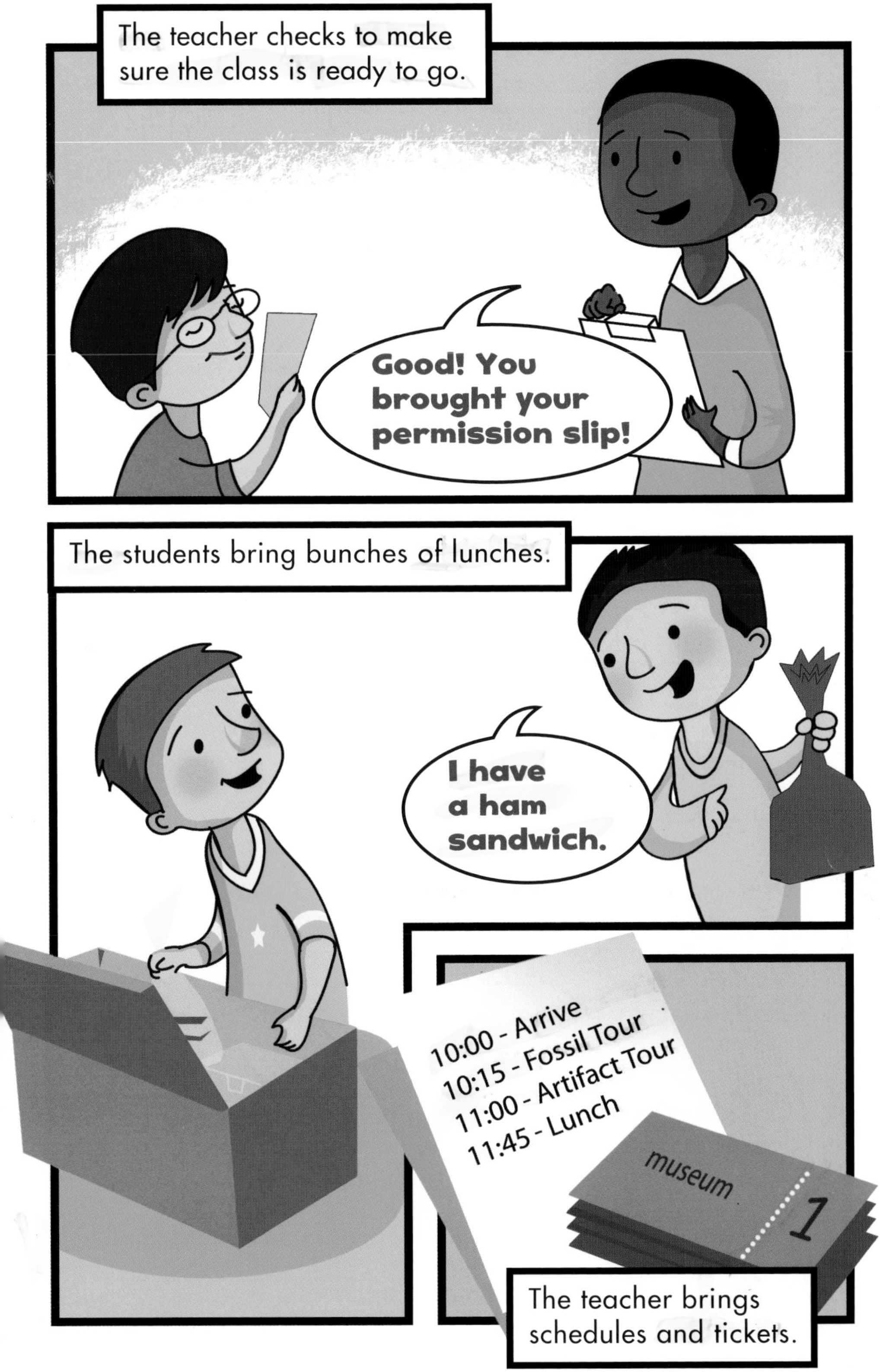
The teacher checks to make sure the class is ready to go.
Good! You brought your permission slip!
The students bring bunches of lunches.
I have a ham sandwich.
10:00 - Arrive
10:15 - Fossil Tour
11:00 - Artifact Tour
11:45 - Lunch
museum
1
The teacher brings schedules and tickets.

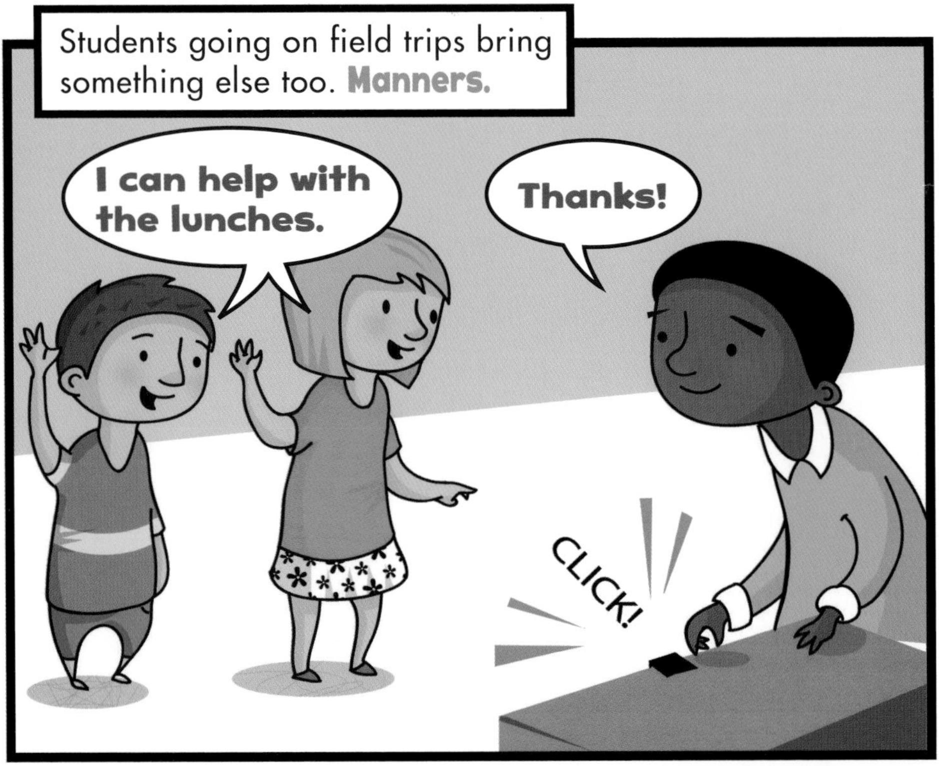
Students going on field trips bring something else too. Manners.
I can help with the lunches.
Thanks!
CLICK!

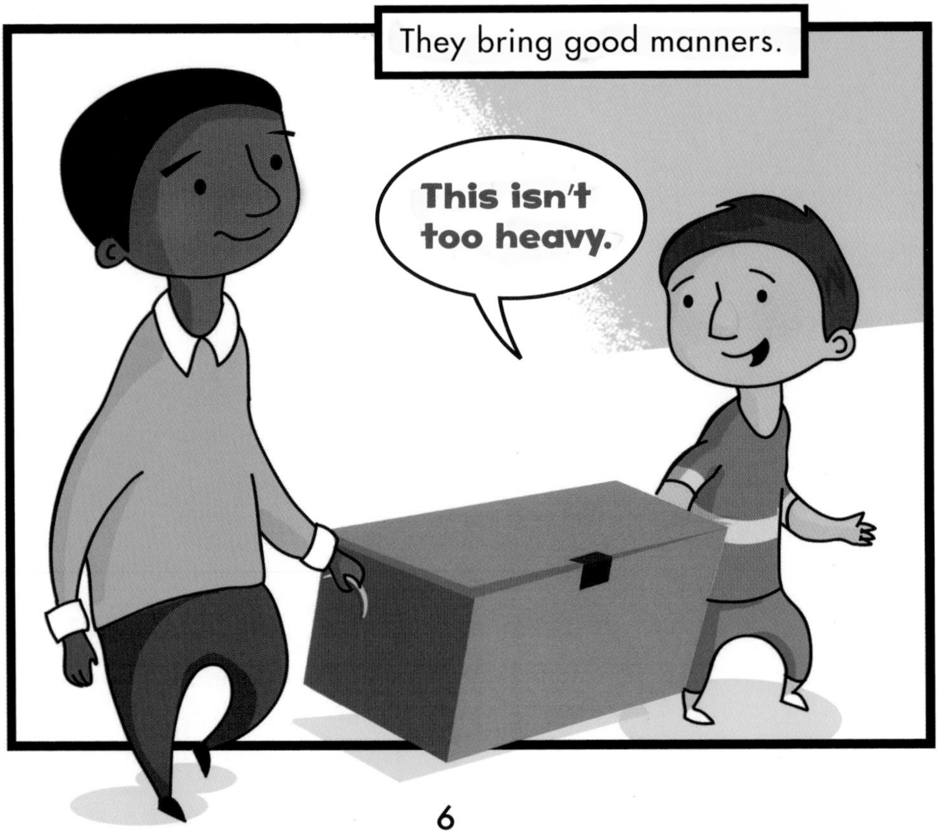
They bring good manners.
This isn't too heavy.

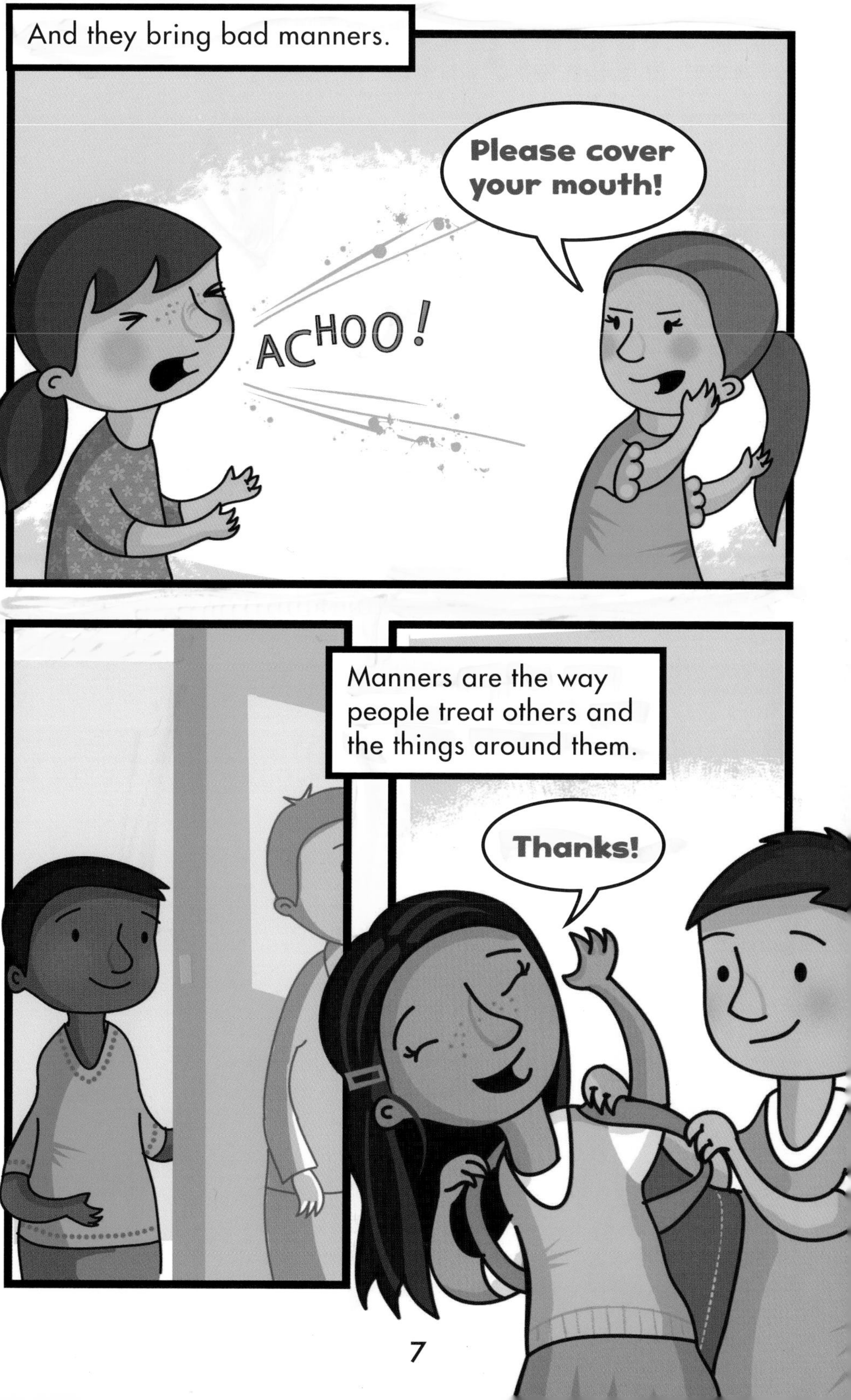
And they bring bad manners.
ACHOO!
Please cover your mouth!
Manners are the way people treat others and the things around them.
Thanks!

All Aboard!

Where do manners start on a field trip? At the museum?

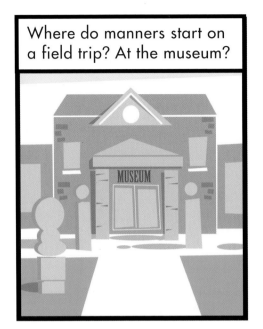

On the bus?

Manners on a field trip start before people even get on the bus.

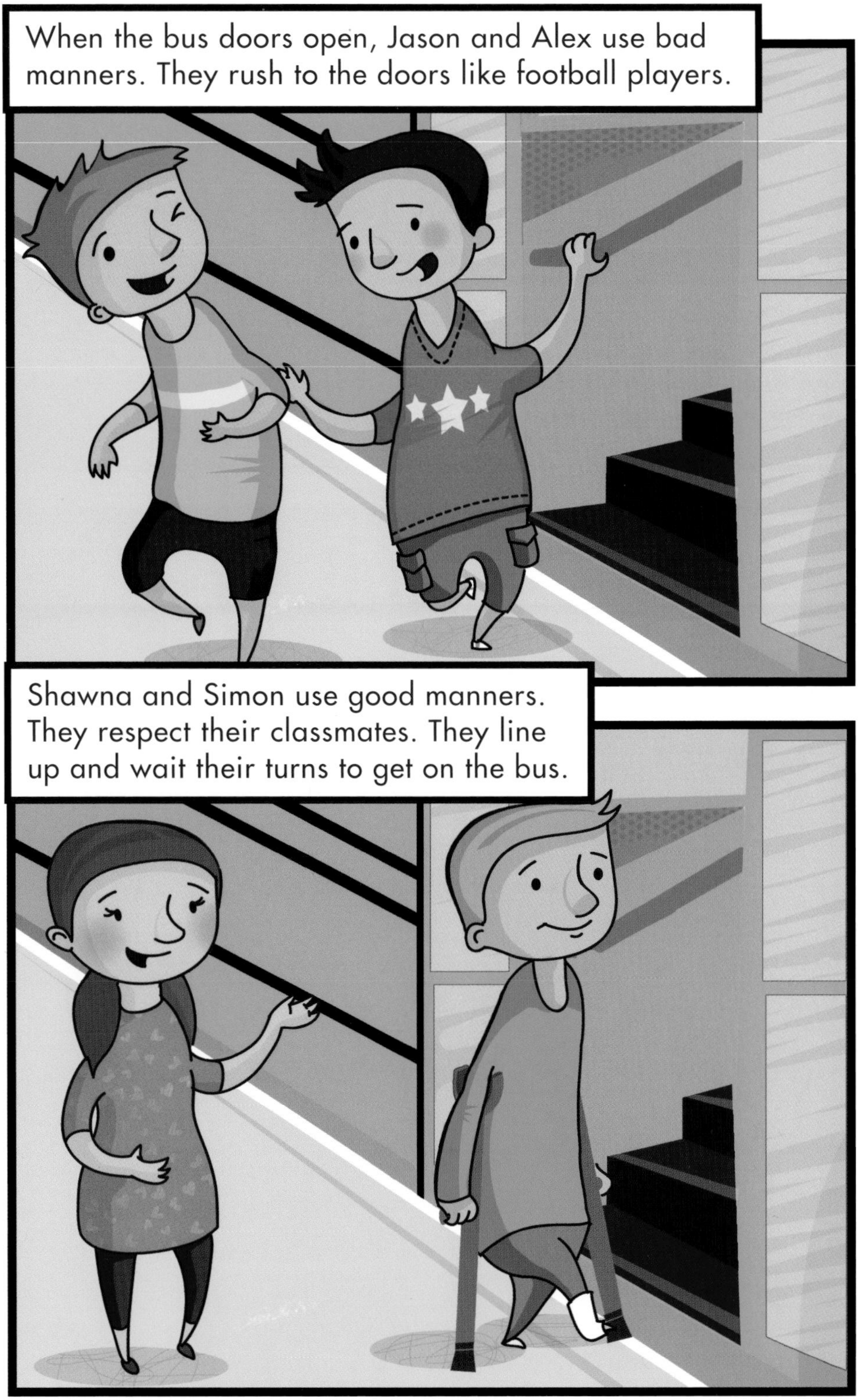
When the bus doors open, Jason and Alex use bad manners. They rush to the doors like football players.
Shawna and Simon use good manners. They respect their classmates. They line up and wait their turns to get on the bus.

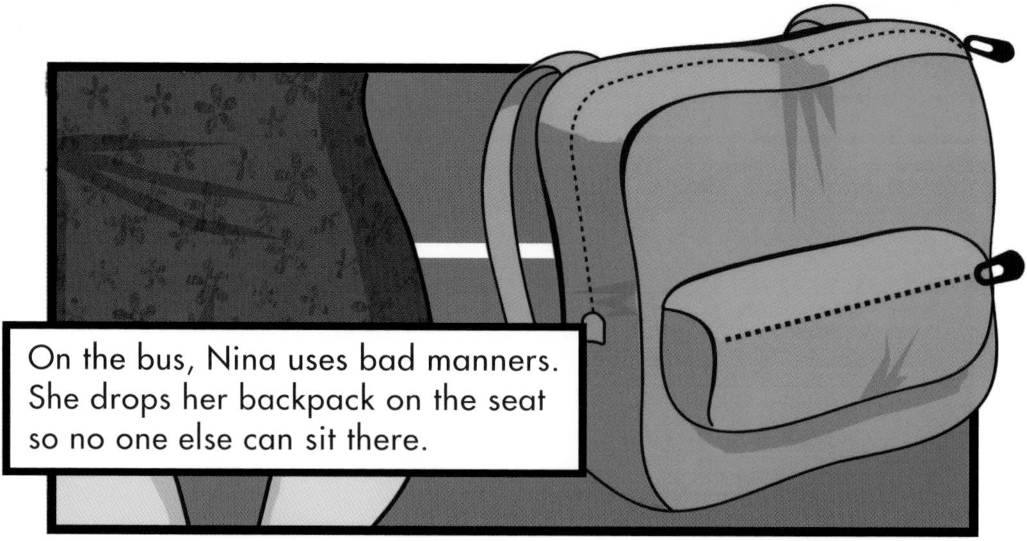
On the bus, Nina uses bad manners. She drops her backpack on the seat so no one else can sit there.

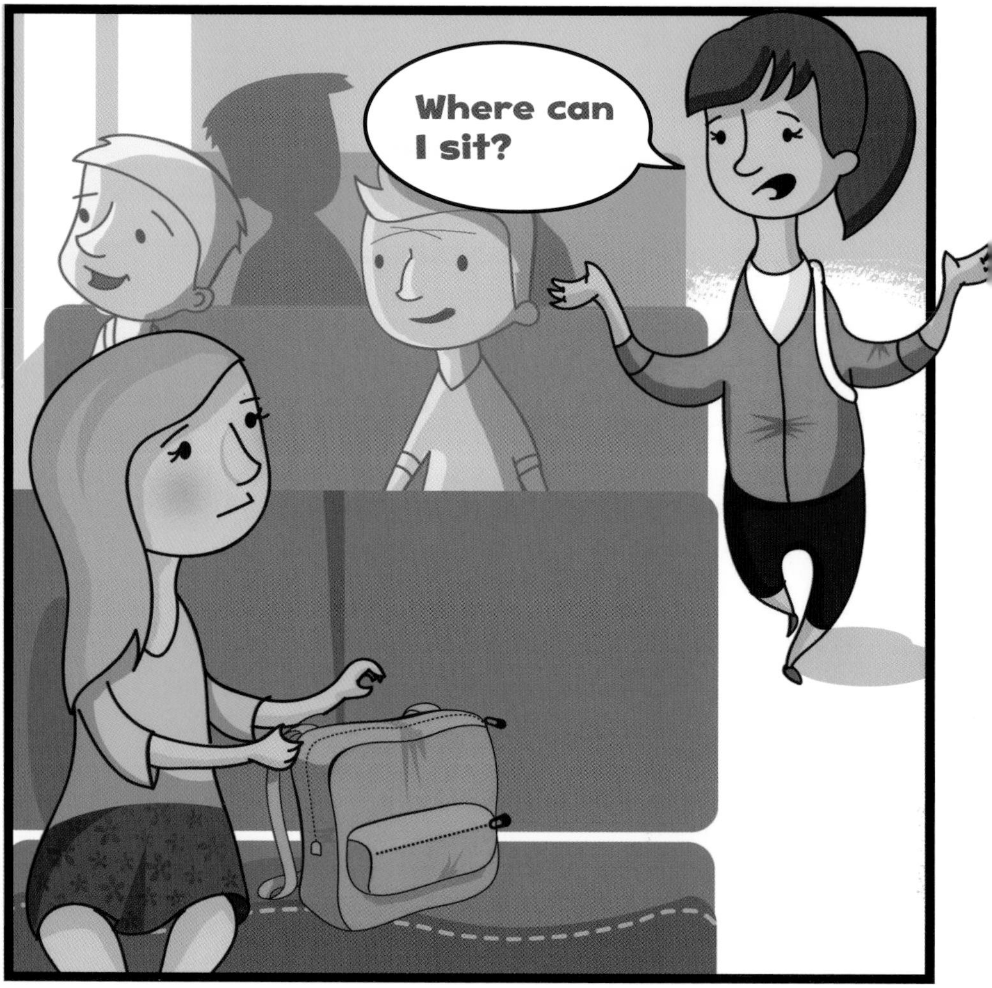
Where can I sit?

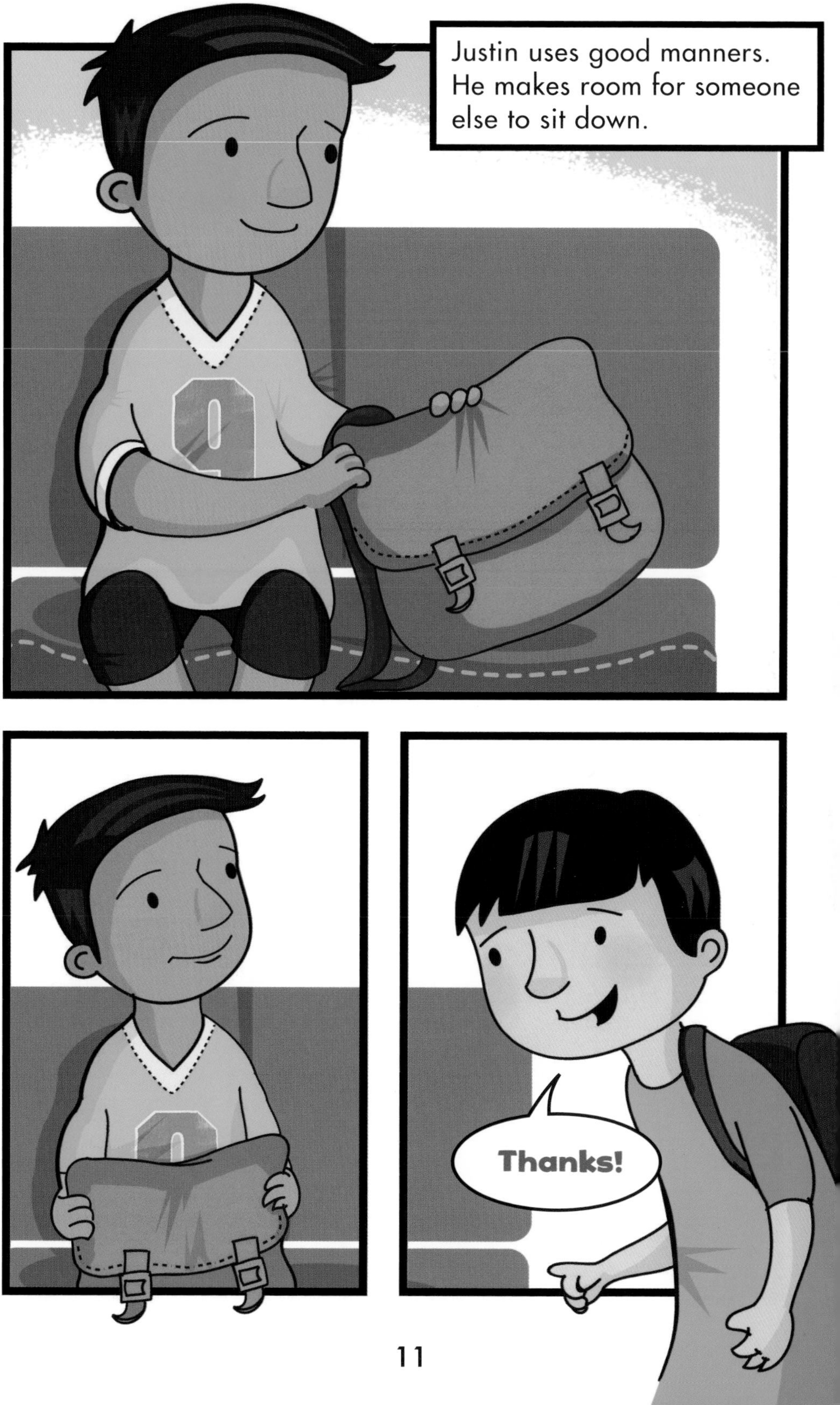
Justin uses good manners.
He makes room for someone
else to sit down.
Thanks!

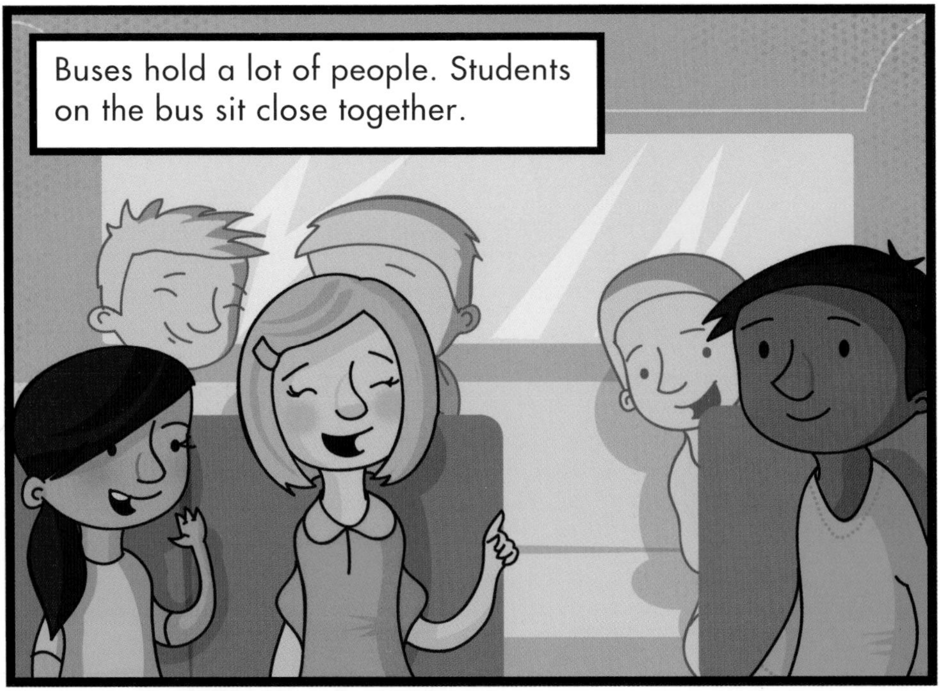
Buses hold a lot of people. Students on the bus sit close together.

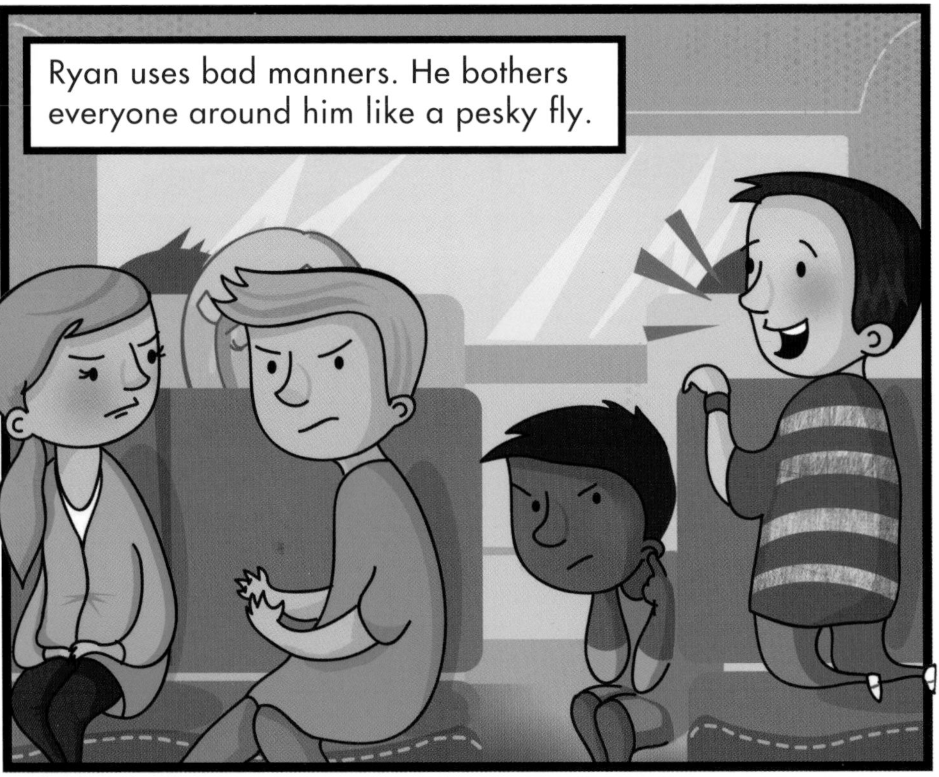
Ryan uses bad manners. He bothers everyone around him like a pesky fly.

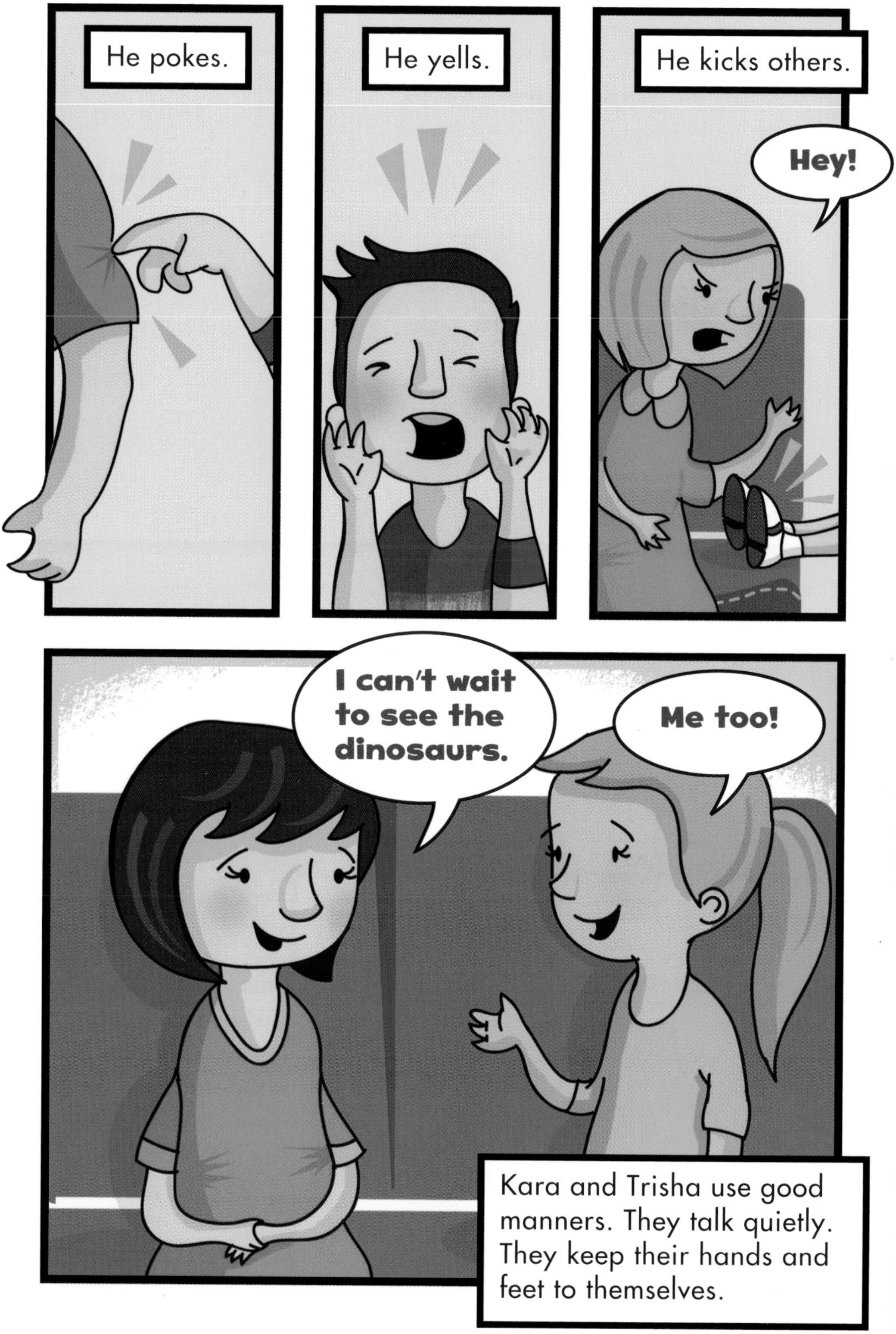
He pokes.
He yells.
He kicks others.
Hey!
I can't wait to see the dinosaurs.
Me too!
Kara and Trisha use good manners. They talk quietly. They keep their hands and feet to themselves.

WE'RE HERE!

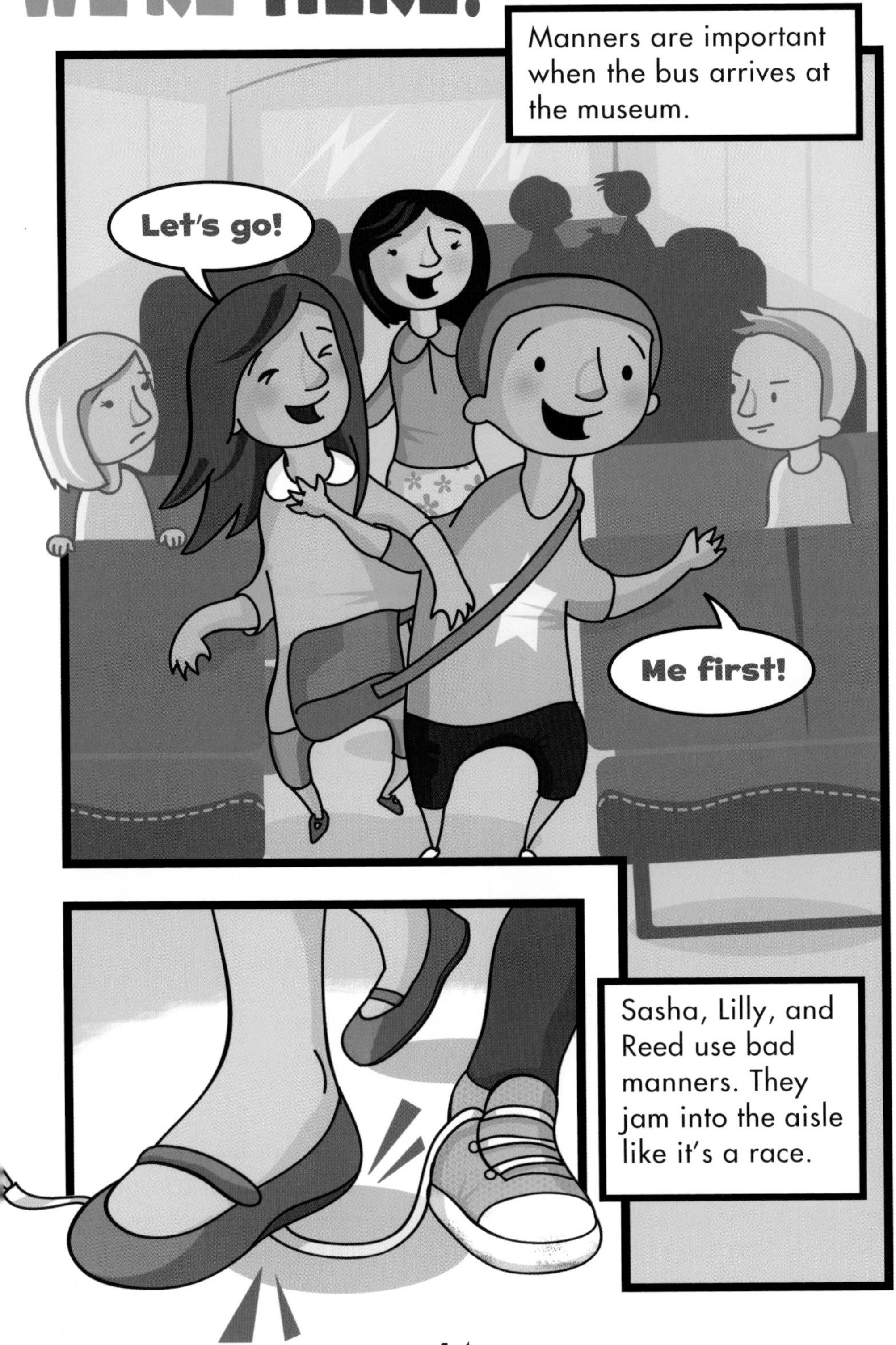
Manners are important when the bus arrives at the museum.
Let's go!
Me first!
Sasha, Lilly, and Reed use bad manners. They jam into the aisle like it's a race.

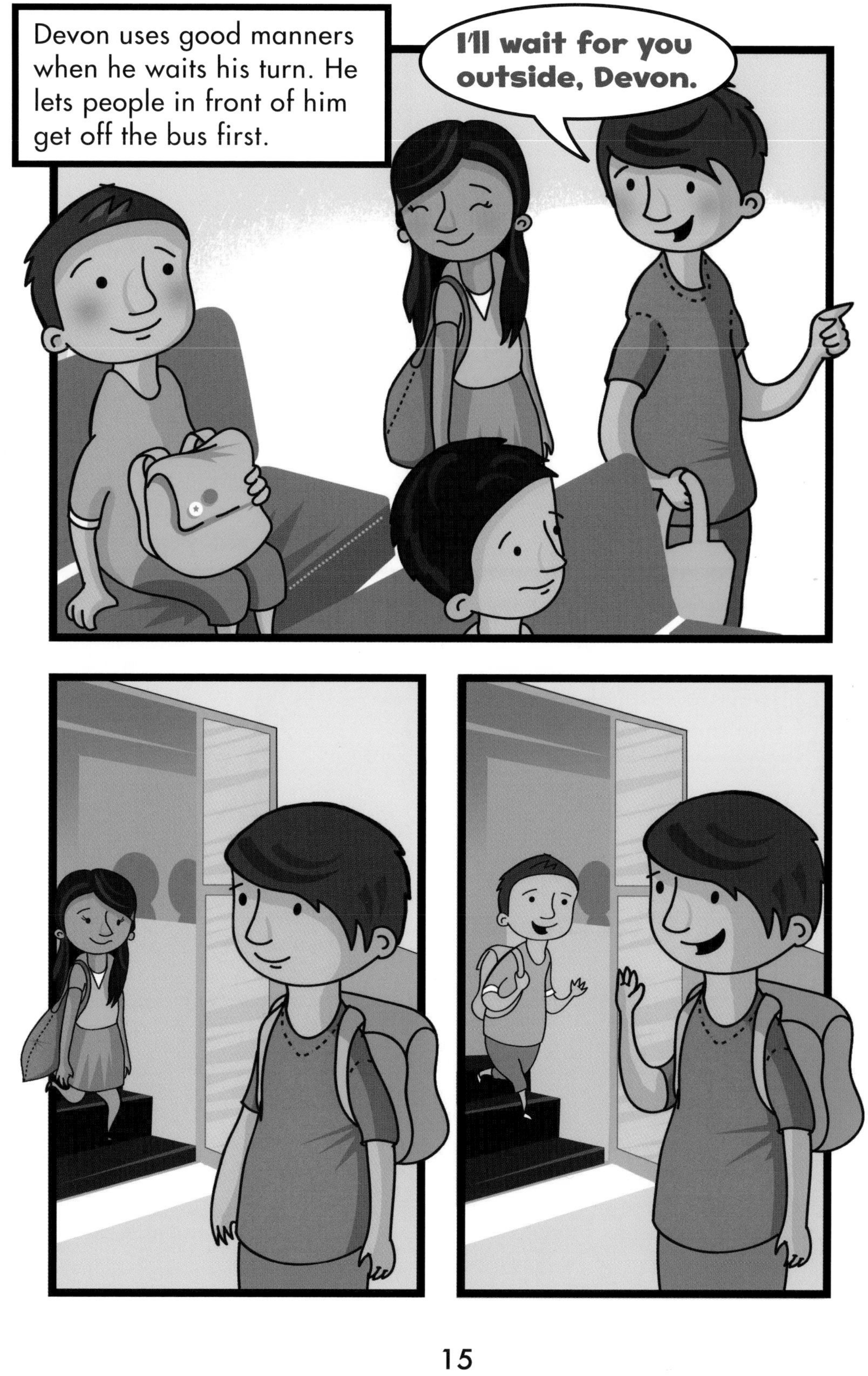
Devon uses good manners when he waits his turn. He lets people in front of him get off the bus first.
I'll wait for you outside, Devon.

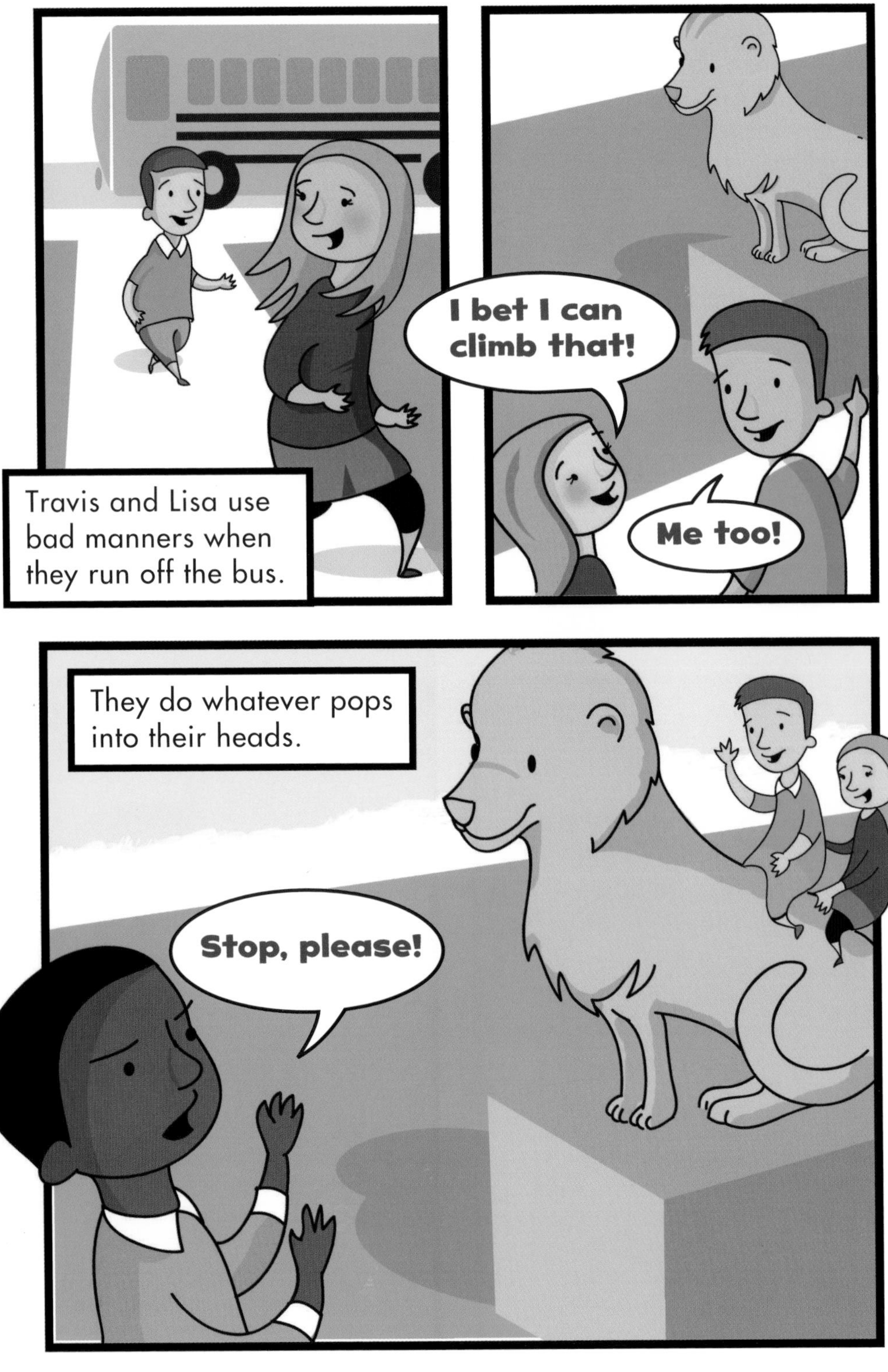
Travis and Lisa use bad manners when they run off the bus.
I bet I can climb that!
Me too!
They do whatever pops into their heads.
Stop, please!

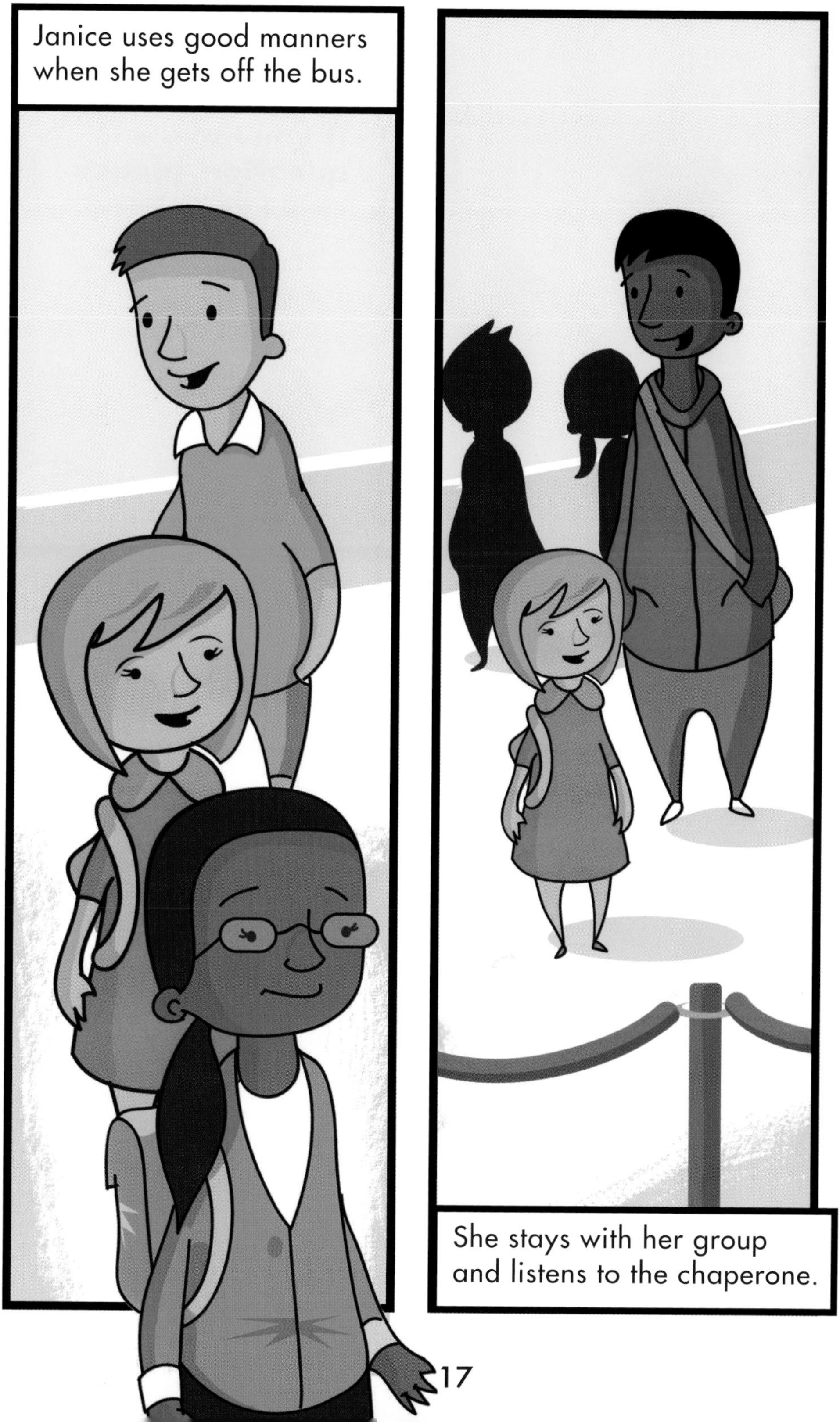
Janice uses good manners when she gets off the bus.
She stays with her group and listens to the chaperone.

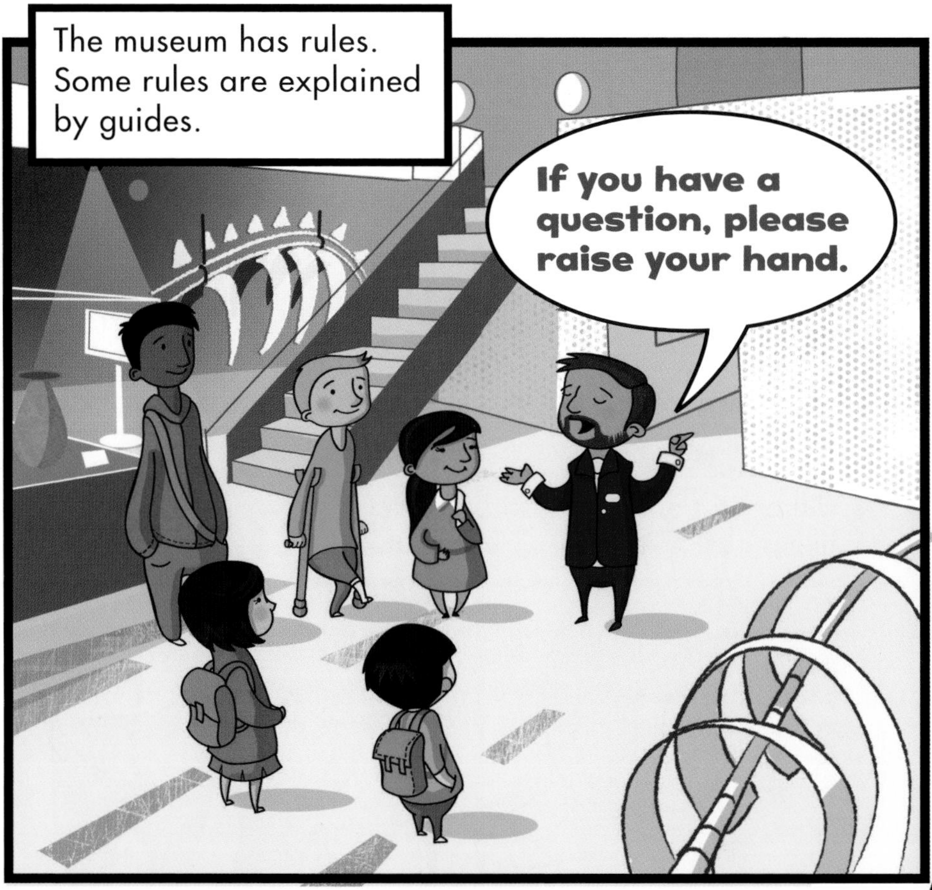
The museum has rules. Some rules are explained by guides.
If you have a question, please raise your hand.

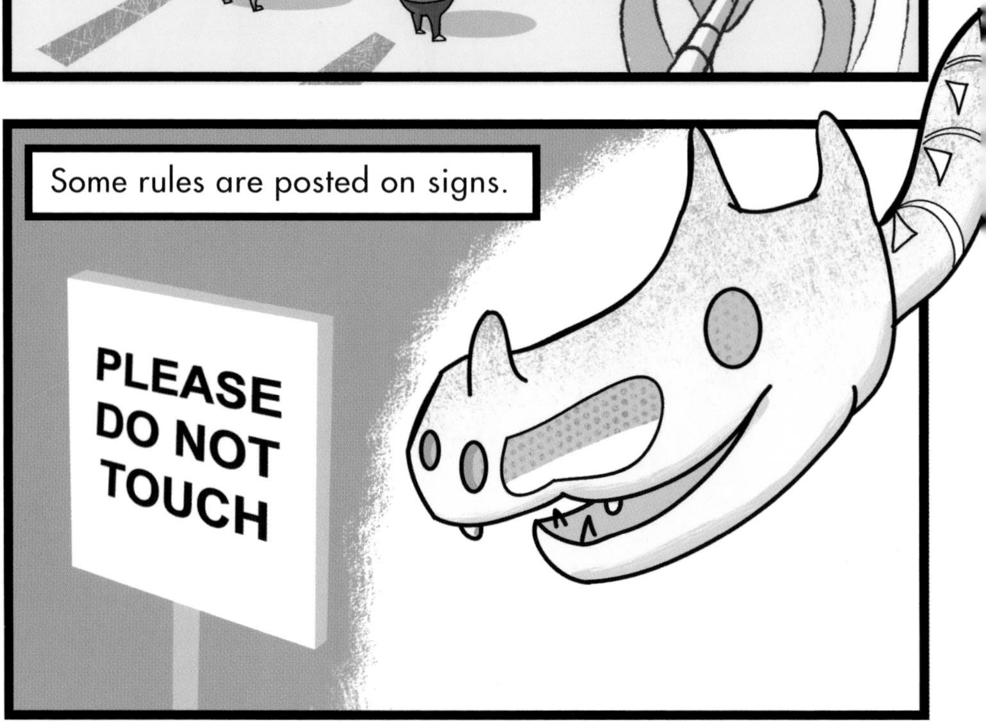
Some rules are posted on signs.
PLEASE DO NOT TOUCH

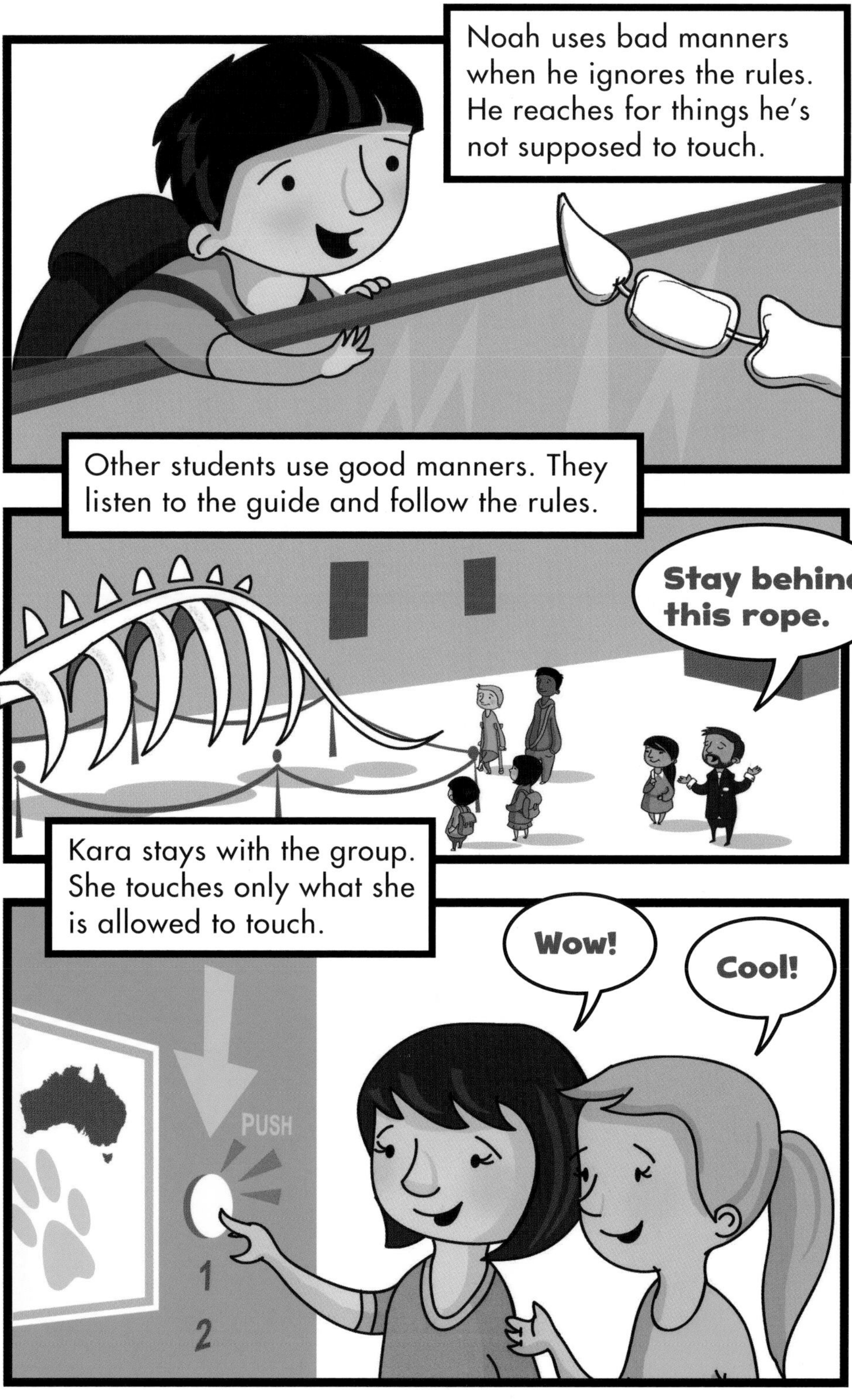
Noah uses bad manners when he ignores the rules. He reaches for things he's not supposed to touch.
Other students use good manners. They listen to the guide and follow the rules.
Stay behind this rope.
Kara stays with the group. She touches only what she is allowed to touch.
Wow!
Cool!
PUSH
1
2

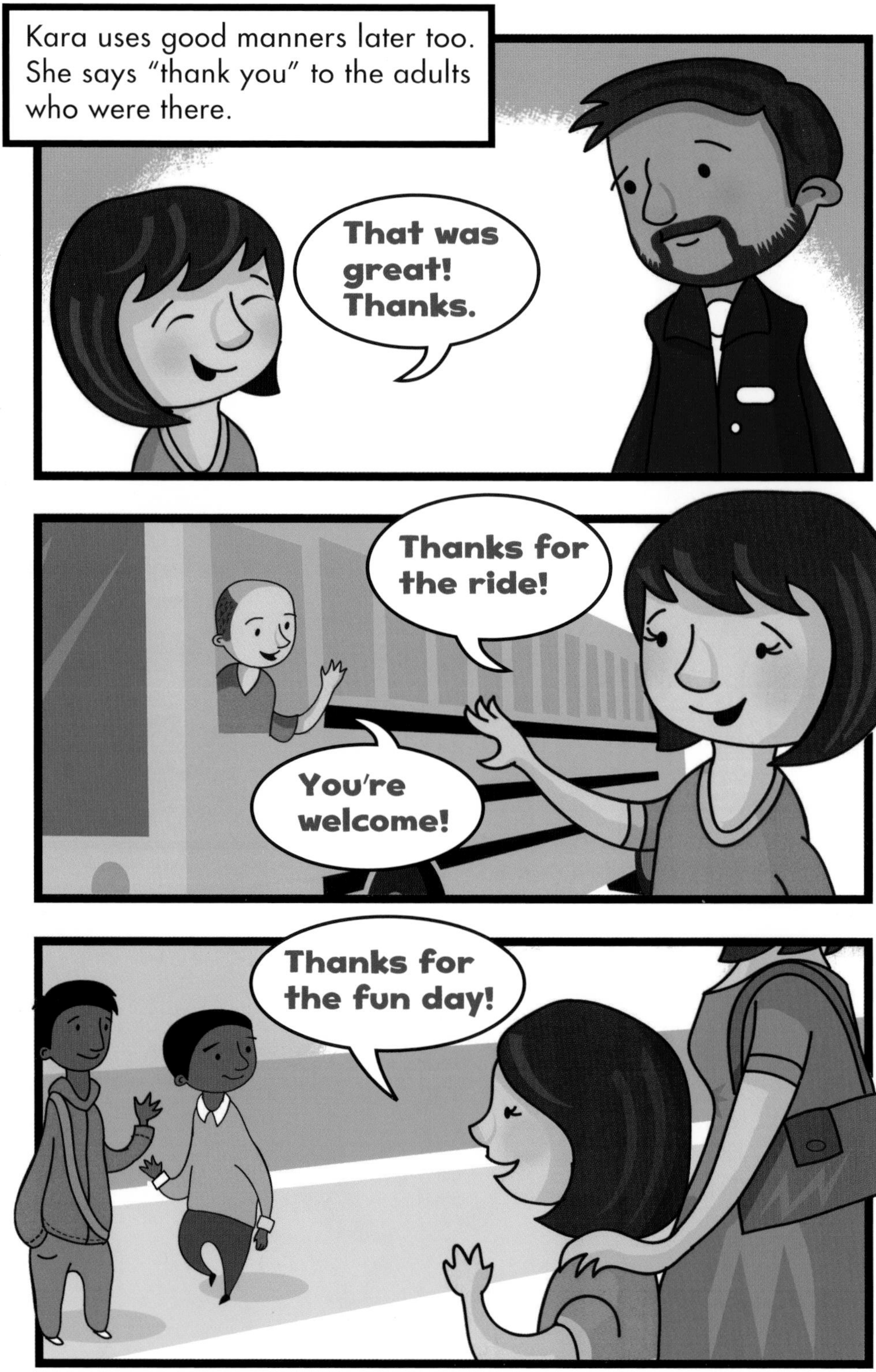
Kara uses good manners later too. She says "thank you" to the adults who were there.
That was great! Thanks.
Thanks for the ride!
You're welcome!
Thanks for the fun day!

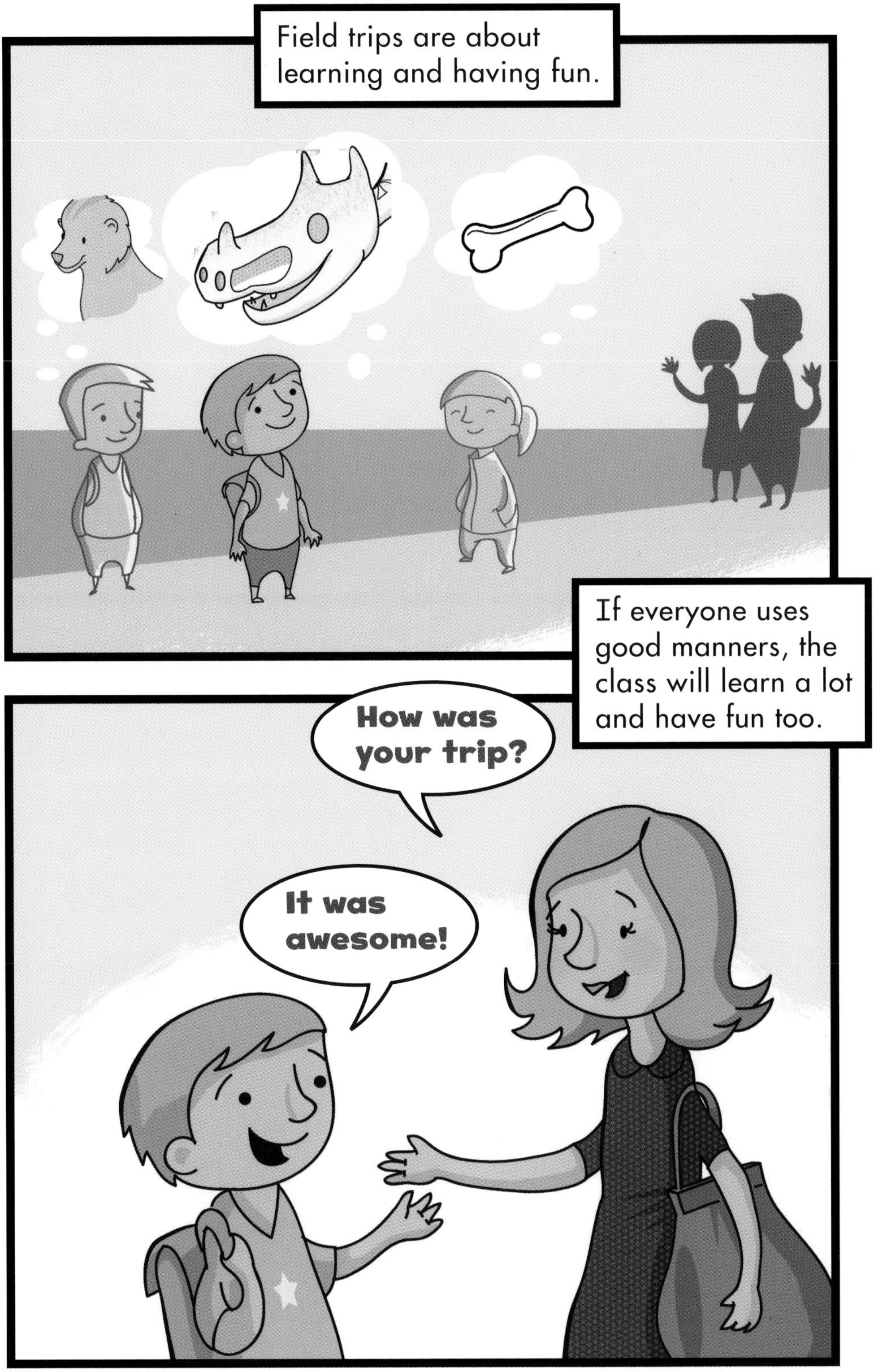
Field trips are about learning and having fun.
If everyone uses good manners, the class will learn a lot and have fun too.
How was your trip?
It was awesome!

GLOSSARY

aisle—a walkway between seats

chaperone—a person who goes with a person or group and looks after them

classmate—someone who is in the same class

guide—a person who shows others around a place or area

museum—a place where objects of art, history, or science are shown

respect—to show you care; respect means to treat others the way you would like to be treated

schedule—a plan of times and places

READ MORE

Finn, Carrie. *Manners at School.* Way to Be!
Minneapolis: Picture Window Books, 2007.

Keller, Laurie. *Do Unto Otters: A Book about
Manners.* New York: Henry Holt, 2007.

Sierra, Judy. *Mind Your Manners, B. B. Wolf.*
New York: Knopf, 2007.

Tourville, Amanda Doering. *Manners on the School
Bus.* Way to Be! Minneapolis: Picture Window
Books, 2009.

INTERNET SITES

FactHound offers a safe, fun way to find Internet
sites related to this book. All of the sites on
FactHound have been researched by our staff.

Here's all you do:

Visit *www.facthound.com*

Type in this code: 9781429653312

Super-cool stuff!

Check out projects, games and lots more at
www.capstonekids.com

INDEX

FIRST GRAPHICS

Manners Matter

TITLES IN THIS SET:

MANNERS MATTER IN THE CLASSROOM

MANNERS MATTER IN THE LIBRARY

MANNERS MATTER ON A FIELD TRIP

MANNERS MATTER ON THE PLAYGROUND